Operations with Fractions

Randall I. Charles
Consultant

Professor Emeritus
Department of Mathematics and
Computer Science
San Jose State University
San Jose, California

Glenview, Illinois
Needham, Massachusetts
Upper Saddle River, New Jersey

Staff Credits

Barbara Albright, Janet Fauser, Brian Kane, Marie Mathis, Sandra Morris, Cindy Noftle, Angie Seltzer, David B. Spangler, Jeff Weidenaar

Additional Credits

Steve Curtis Design, Inc., Barbara Hardt, Anne S. Ryan, Stet Graphics, Inc., Ziebka Editorial Services

ISBN: 0-13-043872-3

14   09

Operations with Fractions

Table of Contents

SKILL 1: Estimating Sums and Differences

To estimate sums and differences of fractions and mixed numbers, round fractions to the nearest whole number. If the fraction is greater than or equal to $\frac{1}{2}$, round the fraction to 1. If it is not, round the fraction to 0.

Example 1

Estimate: $\frac{7}{12} + \frac{1}{4}$.

Compare each fraction to $\frac{1}{2}$.	Round each fraction to either 0 or 1.	Add.
$\frac{7}{12} \geq \frac{1}{2}$	$\frac{7}{12}$ rounds to 1.	1
$\frac{1}{4} < \frac{1}{2}$	$\frac{1}{4}$ rounds to 0.	$\dfrac{+\ 0}{1}$

So, $\frac{7}{12} + \frac{1}{4}$ is about 1.

Example 2

Estimate: $3\frac{8}{15} - 1\frac{5}{6}$.

Compare each fraction to $\frac{1}{2}$.	Round each fraction to either 0 or 1.	Add the rounded fraction to the whole number.	Subtract.
$\frac{8}{15} \geq \frac{1}{2}$	$\frac{8}{15}$ rounds to 1.	$3 + 1 = 4$	4
$\frac{5}{6} \geq \frac{1}{2}$	$\frac{5}{6}$ rounds to 1.	$1 + 1 = 2$	$\dfrac{-\ 2}{2}$

So, $3\frac{8}{15} - 1\frac{5}{6}$ is about 2.

Guided Practice.

Estimate. Remember $\geq$ means "is greater than or equal to."

1. $\frac{7}{9} - \frac{1}{12}$

    a. Is $\frac{7}{9} \geq \frac{1}{2}$? _____

    b. Round $\frac{7}{9}$. _____

    c. Is $\frac{1}{12} \geq \frac{1}{2}$? _____

    d. Round $\frac{1}{12}$. _____

    e. Estimate the difference: _____ – _____ = _____

2. $7\frac{3}{8} + 3\frac{21}{26}$

    a. Is $\frac{3}{8} \geq \frac{1}{2}$? _____

    b. Round $7\frac{3}{8}$. _____

    c. Is $\frac{21}{26} \geq \frac{1}{2}$? _____

    d. Round $3\frac{21}{26}$. _____

    e. Estimate the sum: _____ + _____ = _____

SKILL 1: Practice

Round each fraction to 0 or 1.

1. $\frac{8}{9}$ _____

2. $\frac{2}{15}$ _____

3. $\frac{5}{12}$ _____

4. $\frac{4}{27}$ _____

5. $\frac{7}{15}$ _____

6. $\frac{9}{11}$ _____

7. $\frac{3}{50}$ _____

8. $\frac{23}{25}$ _____

Round each mixed number to the nearest whole number.

9. $2\frac{1}{5}$ _____

10. $3\frac{4}{9}$ _____

11. $4\frac{7}{8}$ _____

12. $1\frac{11}{12}$ _____

13. $3\frac{9}{10}$ _____

14. $7\frac{6}{11}$ _____

15. $2\frac{2}{9}$ _____

16. $5\frac{4}{7}$ _____

Estimate each sum or difference.

17. $8\frac{7}{9} - 1\frac{2}{15}$ _____

18. $\frac{1}{8} + \frac{5}{9}$ _____

19. $\frac{2}{11} + \frac{3}{20}$ _____

20. $2\frac{1}{4} + \frac{11}{12}$ _____

21. $5\frac{1}{8} - 2\frac{13}{16}$ _____

22. $\frac{7}{8} - \frac{7}{9}$ _____

23. $6\frac{7}{9} + 1\frac{2}{15}$ _____

24. $\frac{9}{10} - \frac{2}{9}$ _____

25. $3\frac{10}{11} + 5\frac{3}{4}$ _____

26. $\frac{2}{5} + \frac{7}{12}$ _____

27. $4\frac{8}{15} - \frac{7}{9}$ _____

28. $3\frac{3}{15} + 2\frac{1}{10}$ _____

Solve.

29. Cal had $8\frac{3}{8}$ yards of fabric. He used $6\frac{5}{6}$ yards to reupholster a chair. About how much fabric does he have left? _____

30. Luisa has $3\frac{1}{5}$ cups of apple juice and $2\frac{2}{3}$ cups of cherry cider. About how much fruit drink can she make? _____

TEST PREP

31. Which of the following is the best estimate of $\frac{7}{8} + 4\frac{1}{6}$?

    Skill 1

    A 4

    C 5

    B $4\frac{1}{2}$

    D $5\frac{1}{2}$

32. Which of the following is the best estimate of $8\frac{5}{12} - 1\frac{2}{15}$?

    Skill 1

    F 6

    H 7

    G $6\frac{1}{2}$

    J 9

Section A: Adding and Subtracting Fractions

SKILL 2: Adding Fractions with Like Denominators

Two fractions with the same denominator have **like denominators**.

When adding fractions with like denominators, the denominator acts like a label. It tells you how many equal-size pieces make up a whole. The numerators are the number of pieces you add.

Example 1

Add: $\frac{5}{8} + \frac{1}{8}$. **Write the sum in simplest form.**

Add numerators only.

The denominators do not change.

Write in simplest form.

$$\frac{5}{8} + \frac{1}{8} = \frac{5+1}{8}$$
$$= \frac{6}{8}$$
$$= \frac{3}{4}$$

So, $\frac{5}{8} + \frac{1}{8} = \frac{3}{4}$.

Example 2

Add: $\frac{5}{6} + \frac{3}{6}$. **Write the sum in the simplest form.**

Add the numerators only.

The denominators do not change.

Write in simplest form.

Write as a mixed number.

$$\frac{5}{6} + \frac{3}{6} = \frac{5+3}{6}$$
$$= \frac{8}{6}$$
$$= \frac{8 \div 2}{6 \div 2}$$
$$= \frac{4}{3}$$

$$3\overline{)4}\;\;{}^{1\frac{1}{3}} \atop \begin{array}{c}\underline{3}\\1\end{array}$$

To change $\frac{4}{3}$ to a mixed number, divide 4 by 3.

So, $\frac{5}{6} + \frac{3}{6} = 1\frac{1}{3}$.

Guided Practice

Find each sum in simplest form.

1. $\frac{5}{12} + \frac{5}{12} = \frac{\square + \square}{12} = $ _____ = _____

2. $\frac{7}{8} + \frac{3}{8} = \frac{\square + \square}{8} = $ _____ = _____ = _____

3. $\frac{1}{5} + \frac{2}{5} = $ _____

4. $\frac{5}{9} + \frac{6}{9} = $ _____

5. $\frac{13}{24} + \frac{5}{24} = $ _____

SKILL 2: Practice

Find each sum in simplest form.

1. $\frac{3}{20} + \frac{1}{20} =$ _____

2. $\frac{6}{15} + \frac{4}{15} =$ _____

3. $\frac{3}{4} + \frac{3}{4} =$ _____

4. $\frac{6}{8} + \frac{3}{8} =$ _____

5. $\frac{2}{13} + \frac{3}{13} =$ _____

6. $\frac{6}{8} + \frac{5}{8} =$ _____

7. $\frac{3}{15} + \frac{10}{15} =$ _____

8. $\frac{8}{10} + \frac{4}{10} =$ _____

9. $\frac{7}{14} + \frac{3}{14} =$ _____

10. $\frac{1}{4} + \frac{1}{4} =$ _____

11. $\frac{6}{7} + \frac{1}{7} =$ _____

12. $\frac{14}{19} + \frac{5}{19} =$ _____

13. $\frac{5}{6} + \frac{5}{6} =$ _____

14. $\frac{2}{3} + \frac{1}{3} =$ _____

15. $\frac{15}{18} + \frac{4}{18} =$ _____

16. $\frac{10}{15} + \frac{6}{15} =$ _____

17. $\frac{7}{11} + \frac{3}{11} =$ _____

18. $\frac{4}{10} + \frac{6}{10} =$ _____

19. $\frac{2}{4} + \frac{3}{4} =$ _____

20. $\frac{13}{20} + \frac{5}{20} =$ _____

21. $\frac{1}{4} + \frac{2}{4} =$ _____

22. $\frac{5}{6} + \frac{1}{6} =$ _____

23. $\frac{2}{5} + \frac{4}{5} =$ _____

24. $\frac{5}{9} + \frac{8}{9} =$ _____

Each of the 14 guests at Tony's birthday party brought a gift. The bar graph shows the types of gifts that Tony received. Use the graph for Exercises 25–27. Write each answer in simplest form.

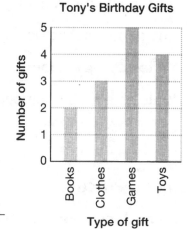

Tony's Birthday Gifts

25. What fraction of the gifts were books or games? _____

26. What fraction of the gifts were clothes, games, or toys? _____

27. What fraction of the guests brought books or toys? _____

28. Find $\frac{7}{12} + \frac{3}{12}$ in simplest form.

Skill 2

A $\frac{1}{2}$ C $\frac{5}{4}$

B $\frac{2}{3}$ D $\frac{5}{6}$

29. Which of the following is the best estimate of $5\frac{1}{9} - 2\frac{7}{8}$?

Skill 1

F 2 H 3

G 4 J 7

SKILL 3: Adding Fractions with Unlike Denominators

Two fractions with different denominators have **unlike denominators**. To add fractions with unlike denominators, change them to equivalent fractions with the same denominator.

You can find equivalent fractions by either multiplying or dividing the numerator and the denominator of a fraction by the same nonzero number. The **least common denominator (LCD)** of two fractions is the least common multiple of the two denominators.

Example

Add: $\frac{3}{4} + \frac{1}{2}$. **Write the sum in simplest form.**

Find the least common denominator for $\frac{3}{4}$ and $\frac{1}{2}$ by listing multiples of both denominators.

Multiples of 4: **4**, 8, 12, 16
Multiples of 2: 2, **4**, 6, 8

The least common multiple of 4 and 2 is 4. So, 4 is also the least common denominator. Only $\frac{1}{2}$ needs to be changed to an equivalent fraction (since $\frac{3}{4}$ already has a denominator of 4).

Multiply the numerator and denominator by 2 to make the denominator 4.

$$\frac{1}{2} = \frac{1 \times 2}{2 \times 2} = \frac{2}{4}$$

Add using the equivalent fractions.
Check that the sum is in the simplest form.

$$\frac{3}{4} \rightarrow \frac{3}{4}$$
$$+\frac{1}{2} \rightarrow \frac{2}{4}$$
$$\overline{\qquad \frac{5}{4} = 1\frac{1}{4}}$$

So, $\frac{3}{4} + \frac{1}{2} = 1\frac{1}{4}$.

Guided Practice

Find $\frac{5}{12} + \frac{5}{8}$ in simplest form.

1. Find the least common multiple of 12 and 8. _____

2. Write as equivalent fractions. $\frac{5}{12} = \frac{\Box}{\Box}$; $\frac{5}{8} = \frac{\Box}{\Box}$

3. Add.

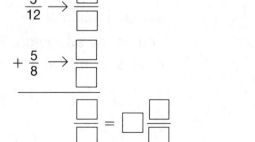

SKILL 3: Practice

Find each sum in simplest form.

1. $\dfrac{1}{2}$
    $+\dfrac{3}{8}$

2. $\dfrac{1}{12}$
    $+\dfrac{3}{4}$

3. $\dfrac{5}{8}$
    $+\dfrac{1}{4}$

4. $\dfrac{5}{6}$
    $+\dfrac{1}{8}$

5. $\dfrac{1}{2}$
    $+\dfrac{2}{5}$

6. $\dfrac{5}{9}$
    $+\dfrac{2}{3}$

7. $\dfrac{3}{4}$
    $+\dfrac{2}{5}$

8. $\dfrac{7}{12}$
    $+\dfrac{1}{3}$

9. $\dfrac{3}{4}$
    $+\dfrac{1}{10}$

10. $\dfrac{1}{3}$
    $+\dfrac{5}{6}$

11. $\dfrac{2}{9}$
    $+\dfrac{1}{6}$

12. $\dfrac{2}{9}$
    $+\dfrac{1}{5}$

13. $\dfrac{3}{5}$
    $+\dfrac{1}{10}$

14. $\dfrac{4}{5}$
    $+\dfrac{1}{3}$

15. $\dfrac{5}{12}$
    $+\dfrac{2}{3}$

16. $\dfrac{2}{3}$
    $+\dfrac{1}{6}$

17. $\dfrac{11}{12}$
    $+\dfrac{1}{6}$

18. $\dfrac{7}{9}$
    $+\dfrac{1}{3}$

19. $\dfrac{3}{4}$
    $+\dfrac{2}{3}$

20. $\dfrac{1}{9}$
    $+\dfrac{5}{6}$

Solve.

21. Lisa spends $\dfrac{1}{5}$ of an hour doing her math homework and $\dfrac{1}{3}$ of an hour doing her social studies homework. What fraction of an hour does she spend doing her math and social studies homework? _____

22. Clint rode his bike $\dfrac{3}{8}$ mile to the library and then $\dfrac{3}{4}$ mile to the park. How far did he ride altogether? _____

23. Find $\dfrac{5}{6} + \dfrac{1}{4}$ in simplest form.

    Skill 3

    A $\dfrac{2}{5}$ **C** $1\dfrac{1}{4}$

    B $\dfrac{11}{12}$ **D** $1\dfrac{1}{12}$

24. Kelly writes for $\dfrac{3}{10}$ of an hour in the morning and $\dfrac{2}{10}$ of an hour in the afternoon. How long does she write in all?

    Skill 2

    F $\dfrac{1}{10}$ h   **H** $\dfrac{1}{5}$ h

    G $\dfrac{1}{2}$ h   **J** $\dfrac{2}{5}$ h

SKILL 4: Adding Mixed Numbers

Just as you can add whole numbers and fractions, you can add mixed numbers.

Example

Find $1\frac{1}{2} + 3\frac{5}{6}$ in simplest form.

The fractions do not have a common denominator.	Rewrite the fractions with a common denominator.	Add the whole numbers. Add the fractions.	Rewrite the improper fraction as a mixed number in simplest form. Add the whole numbers.
$1\frac{1}{2}$ → $+\ 3\frac{5}{6}$	$1\frac{3}{6}$ → $+\ 3\frac{5}{6}$	$1\frac{3}{6}$ → $+\ 3\frac{5}{6}$ ———— $4\frac{8}{6}$	$1\frac{3}{6}$ $+\ 3\frac{5}{6}$ ———— $4\frac{8}{6} = 4 + 1\frac{2}{6}$ $= 4 + 1\frac{1}{3}$ $= 5\frac{1}{3}$

So, $1\frac{1}{2} + 3\frac{5}{6} = 5\frac{1}{3}$.

Guided Practice

Rewrite each number in simplest form.

1. $4\frac{6}{5} = 5\frac{\square}{5}$

2. $12\frac{11}{8} = \square\frac{\square}{8}$

3. $3\frac{6}{4} = 3 + 1\frac{\square}{4} = \square\frac{\square}{\square}$

4. $5\frac{3}{3} = \square$

Add. Write each sum in simplest form.

5. $8\frac{1}{5}$
$+\ 1\frac{2}{5}$
————

6. $2\frac{2}{3}$
$+\ 3\frac{2}{3}$
————

7. $1\frac{1}{2}$
$+\ 1\frac{1}{2}$
————

8. $3\frac{4}{9}$
$+\ 4\frac{7}{9}$
————

9. $4\frac{7}{8}$ → $4\frac{\square}{8}$
$+\ 2\frac{3}{4}$ → $+\ 2\frac{\square}{8}$
————
$6\frac{\square}{8} = 7\frac{\square}{8}$

10. $1\frac{5}{6}$ → $1\frac{\square}{6}$
$+\ 3\frac{2}{3}$ → $+\ 3\frac{\square}{\square}$
————
$4\frac{\square}{\square} = \square\frac{\square}{\square}$

SKILL 4: Practice

Add. Write the sum in simplest form.

1. $13\frac{1}{5}$
    $+ 5\frac{3}{5}$

2. $7\frac{2}{5}$
    $+ 1\frac{2}{3}$

3. $9\frac{20}{23}$
    $+ 14$

4. 6
    $+ 14\frac{1}{2}$

5. 4
    $+ 9\frac{5}{17}$

6. $3\frac{16}{19}$
    $+ 7$

7. $10\frac{13}{15}$
    $+ 4\frac{13}{15}$

8. 2
    $+ 16\frac{5}{19}$

9. $6\frac{1}{7}$
    $+ 19\frac{2}{5}$

10. $15\frac{1}{2}$
    $+ 17\frac{1}{7}$

11. $10\frac{1}{4}$
    $+ 7\frac{3}{4}$

12. $1\frac{4}{5}$
    $+ 3\frac{5}{6}$

13. $11\frac{10}{11}$
    $+ 5$

14. $11\frac{3}{8}$
    $+ 16\frac{3}{4}$

15. $11\frac{4}{5}$
    $+ 2\frac{13}{15}$

16. $16\frac{4}{15}$
    $+ 8\frac{13}{15}$

17. Stephanie used $2\frac{7}{8}$ feet of ribbon to trim a pillowcase and $5\frac{1}{2}$ feet of ribbon to trim a quilt. How much ribbon did she use in all? _____

18. A recipe calls for $1\frac{1}{4}$ cups of cheddar cheese, $1\frac{1}{3}$ cups of Monterey jack cheese, and $1\frac{1}{2}$ cups of mozzarella cheese. How much cheese is used in the recipe? _____

TEST PREP

19. Find the sum in simplest form: $6\frac{2}{3} + 2\frac{4}{9}$.

    Skill 4

    A $8\frac{1}{2}$ **C** $9\frac{1}{9}$

    B $8\frac{3}{5}$ **D** $9\frac{1}{10}$

20. Kyle used $\frac{3}{5}$ yard of wire to hang one painting and $\frac{1}{4}$ yard of wire to hang another painting. How much wire did Kyle use in all?

    Skill 3

    F $\frac{1}{5}$ yd   **H** $\frac{4}{9}$ yd

    G $\frac{3}{20}$ yd   **J** $\frac{17}{20}$ yd

SKILL 5: Subtracting Fractions

To subtract fractions with the same denominator, subtract the numerators and write the difference over the common denominator. Then write the answer in simplest form.

Example 1

Find $\frac{9}{10} - \frac{3}{10}$ in simplest form.

Subtract numerators only.

The denominators do not change.

Write in simplest form.

So, $\frac{9}{10} - \frac{3}{10} = \frac{3}{5}$.

$$\frac{9}{10} - \frac{3}{10} = \frac{9-3}{10}$$
$$= \frac{6}{10}$$
$$= \frac{3}{5}$$

To subtract fractions with unlike denominators, write equivalent fractions with the least common denominator. Then subtract.

Example 2

Find $\frac{7}{15} - \frac{3}{10}$ in simplest form.

The least common multiple of 15 and 10 is 30. Rewrite the fractions using the least common denominator, 30.

$$\frac{7}{15} \rightarrow \frac{7 \times 2}{15 \times 2} \rightarrow \frac{14}{30}$$
$$-\frac{3}{10} \rightarrow \frac{3 \times 3}{10 \times 3} \rightarrow \frac{9}{30}$$

Subtract. Write the difference in simplified form.

$$\frac{14}{30}$$
$$-\frac{9}{30}$$
$$\frac{5}{30} = \frac{1}{6}$$

So, $\frac{7}{15} - \frac{3}{10} = \frac{1}{6}$.

Guided Practice

Find each difference in simplest form.

1. $\frac{5}{6} - \frac{1}{6} = \frac{\Box - \Box}{6} = \frac{\Box}{6} = \frac{\Box}{\Box}$

2. $\frac{7}{10} - \frac{1}{4} = \frac{\Box - \Box}{20} = \frac{\Box}{\Box}$

3. $\frac{2}{3} - \frac{1}{5} = \frac{\Box - \Box}{15} = \frac{\Box}{\Box}$

4. $\frac{17}{18} - \frac{1}{9} = \frac{\Box - \Box}{18} = \frac{\Box}{18} = \frac{\Box}{\Box}$

Name	Date	Class

SKILL 5: Practice

Find each difference in simplest form.

1. $\frac{3}{4}$
    $-\frac{1}{8}$

2. $\frac{6}{8}$
    $-\frac{5}{8}$

3. $\frac{8}{9}$
    $-\frac{2}{3}$

4. $\frac{3}{20}$
    $-\frac{1}{20}$

5. $\frac{5}{6}$
    $-\frac{1}{2}$

6. $\frac{1}{5}$
    $-\frac{1}{7}$

7. $\frac{4}{5}$
    $-\frac{1}{6}$

8. $\frac{7}{14}$
    $-\frac{3}{14}$

9. $\frac{3}{5}$
    $-\frac{1}{3}$

10. $\frac{7}{8}$
    $-\frac{1}{4}$

11. $\frac{2}{5}$
    $-\frac{1}{10}$

12. $\frac{2}{3}$
    $-\frac{1}{4}$

13. $\frac{5}{6}$
    $-\frac{1}{3}$

14. $\frac{2}{3}$
    $-\frac{2}{5}$

15. $\frac{9}{10}$
    $-\frac{3}{4}$

Solve.

16. Josy exercised $\frac{5}{6}$ of an hour on Monday and $\frac{3}{5}$ of an hour on Tuesday. How much longer did she exercise on Monday? _____

17. Larry, Mary, and Sara share a pizza. The fraction of the pizza each ate is shown in the table at the right. Which two children were closest in the fraction they ate?

    _____

Fraction of the Pizza Eaten	
Larry	$\frac{1}{6}$
Mary	$\frac{3}{8}$
Sara	$\frac{11}{24}$

18. Find $\frac{7}{9} - \frac{2}{3}$ in simplest form.

    Skill 5

    A $\frac{1}{9}$ **C** $\frac{5}{9}$

    B $\frac{1}{6}$ **D** $\frac{5}{6}$

19. Find $\frac{3}{5} + 2\frac{3}{4}$ in simplest form.

    Skill 4

    F $2\frac{2}{3}$ **H** $3\frac{3}{20}$

    G $2\frac{7}{20}$ **J** $3\frac{7}{20}$

© Prentice-Hall, Inc.

Section A: Adding and Subtracting Fractions

SKILL 6: Subtracting Mixed Numbers with Like Denominators

Just as you can subtract whole numbers and fractions, you can subtract mixed numbers. If the fraction to be subtracted is larger than the other fraction, you must rename so that the fraction part is 1 more and the whole number part is 1 less.

Example 1

Rename $4\frac{2}{3}$ as $3\frac{?}{3}$.

$4\frac{2}{3}$

Rename 4 as $3 + \frac{3}{3}$. Then add $\frac{2}{3}$.

$4\frac{2}{3} = 3 + \frac{3}{3} + \frac{2}{3} = 3\frac{5}{3}$.

So, $4\frac{2}{3} = 3\frac{5}{3}$.

$3\frac{5}{3}$

Example 2

Find $6\frac{1}{4} - 2\frac{3}{4}$ in simplest form.

Rename $6\frac{1}{4}$ as $5\frac{4}{4} + \frac{1}{4}$, or $5\frac{5}{4}$	Subtract the fractions.	Subtract the whole numbers. Write the difference in simplest form.

$$6\frac{1}{4}$$
$$-\,2\frac{3}{4}$$
___

$$5\frac{5}{4}$$
$$-\,2\frac{3}{4}$$
___

$$5\frac{5}{4}$$
$$-\,2\frac{3}{4}$$
___
$$\frac{2}{4}$$

$$5\frac{5}{4}$$
$$-\,2\frac{3}{4}$$
___
$$3\frac{2}{4} = 3\frac{1}{2}$$

So, $6\frac{1}{4} - 2\frac{3}{4} = 3\frac{1}{2}$.

Guided Practice

Rename each number.

1. $2\frac{4}{5} = 1\frac{\square}{5}$

2. $10\frac{1}{2} = 9\frac{\square}{2}$

3. $16\frac{5}{8} = 15\frac{\square}{8}$

4. $5 = 4\frac{\square}{3}$

Subtract. Write each difference in simplest form.

5. $5\frac{1}{3} \rightarrow 4\frac{\square}{3}$
$\quad -1\frac{2}{3} \quad\quad -1\frac{2}{3}$
___

$\square\frac{\square}{\square}$

6. $8 \rightarrow 7\frac{\square}{5}$
$\quad\quad -3\frac{2}{5} \quad -3\frac{2}{5}$
___

$\square\frac{\square}{\square}$

7. $7\frac{1}{8} \rightarrow 6\frac{\square}{8}$
$\quad -2\frac{5}{8} \quad\quad -2\frac{5}{8}$
___

$\square\frac{\square}{\square} = \square\frac{\square}{\square}$

SKILL 6: Practice

Rename each number.

1. $8 = 7\frac{\square}{5}$

2. $4\frac{1}{8} = 3\frac{\square}{8}$

3. $5\frac{3}{5} = 4\frac{\square}{5}$

4. $3\frac{4}{9} = 2\frac{\square}{9}$

5. $5 = 4\frac{\square}{12}$

6. $9\frac{1}{6} = 8\frac{\square}{6}$

Subtract. Write each difference in simplest form.

7. $\begin{array}{r} 4 \\ -1\frac{2}{3} \\ \hline \end{array}$

8. $\begin{array}{r} 6\frac{1}{4} \\ -4\frac{3}{4} \\ \hline \end{array}$

9. $\begin{array}{r} 5\frac{2}{5} \\ -2\frac{4}{5} \\ \hline \end{array}$

10. $\begin{array}{r} 7 \\ -4\frac{4}{9} \\ \hline \end{array}$

11. $\begin{array}{r} 3\frac{2}{7} \\ -1\frac{6}{7} \\ \hline \end{array}$

12. $\begin{array}{r} 8 \\ -3\frac{3}{4} \\ \hline \end{array}$

13. $\begin{array}{r} 6 \\ -4\frac{5}{8} \\ \hline \end{array}$

14. $\begin{array}{r} 9 \\ -2\frac{1}{2} \\ \hline \end{array}$

15. $\begin{array}{r} 4\frac{1}{8} \\ -1\frac{3}{8} \\ \hline \end{array}$

16. $\begin{array}{r} 12 \\ -3\frac{3}{4} \\ \hline \end{array}$

17. $\begin{array}{r} 5\frac{3}{8} \\ -2\frac{7}{8} \\ \hline \end{array}$

18. $\begin{array}{r} 7 \\ -\frac{5}{6} \\ \hline \end{array}$

19. $6\frac{2}{9} - 3\frac{7}{9} =$ _____

20. $4\frac{1}{12} - 1\frac{5}{12} =$ _____

21. $3 - 2\frac{3}{5} =$ _____

Solve.

22. Caitlin buys 3 pounds of peanuts. She uses $1\frac{7}{8}$ pounds to make some trail mix. How many pounds of peanuts does she have left? _____

23. Brad rode his bike $4\frac{3}{10}$ miles. Then he ran $2\frac{9}{10}$ miles. How much farther did he ride than run? _____

24. Find $12 - 8\frac{2}{3}$ in simplest form.

Skill 6

A $3\frac{1}{3}$ **C** $4\frac{1}{3}$

B $3\frac{2}{3}$ **D** $4\frac{2}{3}$

25. Find $\frac{11}{12} - \frac{7}{12}$ in simplest form.

Skill 5

F $\frac{1}{4}$ **H** $\frac{4}{11}$

G $\frac{1}{3}$ **J** $\frac{4}{7}$

SKILL 7: Subtracting Mixed Numbers with Unlike Denominators

To subtract mixed numbers with unlike denominators, first write equivalent fractions with a common denominator. Sometimes you will need to rename before you can subtract the fractions.

Example 1

Find $3\frac{5}{8} - 1\frac{1}{4}$ in simplest form.

Rewrite the fractions using their LCD, 8.

$3\frac{5}{8} \;\rightarrow\; 3\frac{5}{8}$

$-\,1\frac{1}{4} \;\rightarrow\; 1\frac{2}{8}$

So, $3\frac{5}{8} - 1\frac{1}{4} = 2\frac{3}{8}$.

Subtract the fractions.

$3\frac{5}{8}$

$-\,1\frac{2}{8}$

$\overline{\quad\frac{3}{8}}$

Subtract the whole numbers.

$3\frac{5}{8}$

$-\,1\frac{2}{8}$

$\overline{\;2\frac{3}{8}}$

Example 2

Find $8\frac{1}{3} - 2\frac{5}{6}$ in simplest form.

Rewrite the fractions using their LCD, 6.

$8\frac{1}{3} \;\rightarrow\; 8\frac{2}{6}$

$-\,2\frac{5}{6} \;\rightarrow\; 2\frac{5}{6}$

So, $8\frac{1}{3} - 2\frac{5}{6} = 5\frac{1}{2}$.

Since $\frac{2}{6} < \frac{5}{6}$, rename $8\frac{2}{6}$ as $7\frac{6}{6} + \frac{2}{6}$, or $7\frac{8}{6}$.

$7\frac{8}{6}$

$-\,2\frac{5}{6}$

Subtract the fractions and whole numbers. Write the difference in simplest form.

$7\frac{8}{6}$

$-\,2\frac{5}{6}$

$\overline{\;5\frac{3}{6} = 5\frac{1}{2}}$

Guided Practice

Find each difference in simplest form.

1. $6\frac{1}{5} \;\rightarrow\; 6\frac{\square}{10} \;\rightarrow\; 5\frac{\square}{10}$

$-\,3\frac{7}{10} \;\rightarrow\; -\,3\frac{7}{10} \;\rightarrow\; -\,3\frac{7}{10}$

2. $7\frac{1}{5} \;\rightarrow\; 7\frac{\square}{15} \;\rightarrow\; 6\frac{\square}{15}$

$-\,2\frac{2}{3} \;\rightarrow\; -\,2\frac{\square}{15} \;\rightarrow\; -\,2\frac{\square}{15}$

3. $5\frac{7}{8} - 2\frac{3}{4} = $ _____

4. $6\frac{1}{6} - 3\frac{2}{3} = $ _____

SKILL 7: Practice

Find each difference in simplest form.

1. $5\frac{2}{7}$
    $-4\frac{2}{3}$

2. $15\frac{7}{10}$
    $-12\frac{2}{5}$

3. $7\frac{1}{3}$
    $-4\frac{1}{18}$

4. $2\frac{3}{8}$
    $-2\frac{5}{16}$

5. $8\frac{5}{8}$
    $-4\frac{7}{24}$

6. $10\frac{1}{3}$
    $-4\frac{5}{6}$

7. $9\frac{2}{3}$
    $-1\frac{1}{10}$

8. $12\frac{3}{8}$
    $-8\frac{5}{6}$

9. $5\frac{1}{6}$
    $-2\frac{3}{5}$

10. $9\frac{1}{10}$
    $-7\frac{2}{5}$

11. $3\frac{1}{2}$
    $-1\frac{5}{6}$

12. $3\frac{2}{3}$
    $-1\frac{8}{15}$

13. $10\frac{4}{5}$
    $-1\frac{14}{25}$

14. $8\frac{4}{7}$
    $-1\frac{1}{2}$

15. $2\frac{1}{2}$
    $-1\frac{19}{21}$

16. $12\frac{3}{4}$
    $-5\frac{1}{7}$

17. $7\frac{4}{5}$
    $-2\frac{5}{8}$

18. $10\frac{17}{21}$
    $-1\frac{5}{7}$

19. $10\frac{7}{18}$
    $-4\frac{1}{3}$

20. $15\frac{11}{14}$
    $-14\frac{1}{7}$

Solve.

21. Jessie baked $6\frac{1}{2}$ dozen cookies for a bake sale, and $4\frac{2}{3}$ dozen
    of the cookies were sold. How many dozen cookies were left over? _____

22. Find $6\frac{2}{3} - 3\frac{1}{4}$ in simplest form.

    Skill 7

    A $3\frac{5}{12}$ **C** $4\frac{5}{12}$

    B $3\frac{7}{12}$ **D** $4\frac{7}{12}$

23. Which of the following is the best
    estimate of $2\frac{10}{11} + 3\frac{6}{7}$?

    Skill 1

    F 5   **H** 7

    G 6   **J** 8

SKILL 8: PROBLEM SOLVING: Adding and Subtracting Fractions and Mixed Numbers

You can solve problems with fractions and mixed numbers the same way you solve problems with whole numbers. Sometimes you may have to use more than one operation, or you may have to interpret what the fraction means to solve a problem.

Example

Ada had rehearsals for a dance recital on Friday and on Saturday. On Friday she practiced for $1\frac{1}{3}$ hours and on Saturday she practiced for $1\frac{1}{5}$ hours. On which day did she practice longer? How much longer?

Read Ada spent $1\frac{1}{3}$ hours practicing on Friday and $1\frac{1}{5}$ hours practicing on Saturday.

Plan Compare the mixed numbers and then subtract to find the difference.

Solve Since $\frac{1}{3} > \frac{1}{5}$, $1\frac{1}{3} > 1\frac{1}{5}$. So, she spent more time practicing on Friday than on Saturday.

Subtract:
$$\begin{array}{rcl} 1\frac{1}{3} & \rightarrow & 1\frac{5}{15} \\ -\,1\frac{1}{5} & \rightarrow & -\,1\frac{3}{15} \\ \hline & & \frac{2}{15} \end{array}$$

She practiced $\frac{2}{15}$ hour more on Friday than on Saturday.

Look Back See that your answer makes sense. Estimate the difference. Both fractions round to zero, so the difference is about $1 - 1 = 0$. Since 0 is close to $\frac{2}{15}$, the answer makes sense.

Guided Practice

Jamison walked $1\frac{1}{4}$ miles from his home to the park. He walked around a $\frac{1}{2}$-mile track three times before walking home. How far did he walk altogether?

1. What operation should you use to solve? _____

2. Write the number sentence you can use to find the total distance.

_____

3. How far did he walk altogether? _____

SKILL 8: Practice

Solve each problem.

1. Toni has an art class for $1\frac{1}{3}$ hours every Thursday. She was late to class this Thursday and was in class for $\frac{5}{6}$ of an hour. How late was she to art class?

_____

2. At Paul's Pet Palace, $\frac{3}{16}$ of the animals are dogs and $\frac{5}{24}$ of the animals are cats. What fraction of the animals are neither dogs nor cats?

_____

3. At a school music festival, Julia played saxophone for $2\frac{2}{3}$ hours, Caroline sang for $1\frac{3}{4}$ hours, Lamont played saxophone for $1\frac{1}{4}$ hours, and Taylor sang for $2\frac{3}{8}$ hours. Who had more time, the saxophone players or the singers? How much more?

_____

4. Steve bought $2\frac{3}{4}$ pounds of broccoli, $1\frac{1}{2}$ pounds of spinach, and $\frac{7}{8}$ pound of carrots. He also bought $2\frac{1}{2}$ pounds of apples and $2\frac{3}{8}$ pounds of oranges. Did he buy more fruit or more vegetables? How much more?

_____

5. To get to school, Harley traveled $\frac{5}{6}$ mile along Arlington Avenue, then another $\frac{3}{8}$ mile along Forest Street. How long is his trip?

_____

6. During a trip, Steve drove $\frac{1}{4}$ of the time, Chris drove $\frac{1}{6}$ of the time, and Doris drove the rest of the time. What fraction of the time did Doris drive?

_____

7. Paolo noticed that Channel 8 devoted $\frac{1}{6}$ hour to a news story and Channel 12 devoted $\frac{1}{8}$ hour to the same story. Which channel devoted more time? How much more time?

_____

TEST PREP

8. A recipe calls for $2\frac{1}{3}$ cups of milk plus enough water to make $3\frac{1}{4}$ cups of liquid. How much water is used in the recipe?

Skill 8

A $\frac{1}{3}$ c   **C** $5\frac{2}{7}$ c

B $\frac{11}{12}$ c   **D** $5\frac{7}{12}$ c

9. Find $3\frac{5}{8} + 1\frac{4}{5}$ in simplest form.

Skill 4

F $4\frac{9}{13}$ **H** $4\frac{17}{40}$

G $5\frac{9}{40}$ **J** $5\frac{17}{40}$

Name _____   Date _____   Class _____

Circle each correct answer.

1. Find $\frac{3}{5} + \frac{1}{4}$ in simplest form.

   Skill 3

   A $\frac{1}{5}$ C $\frac{13}{20}$

   B $\frac{4}{9}$ D $\frac{17}{20}$

2. Elaine used $\frac{3}{4}$ cup of orange juice and $\frac{1}{8}$ cup of lemon juice to make some pudding. How much more orange juice than lemon juice did she use?

   Skill 5

   F $\frac{1}{4}$ cup   H $\frac{3}{8}$ cup

   G $\frac{1}{2}$ cup   J $\frac{5}{8}$ cup

3. Which of the following is the best estimate of $1\frac{3}{20} + \frac{9}{10}$?

   Skill 1

   A 0   C 2

   B 1   D 3

4. Find $\frac{9}{10} - \frac{2}{5}$ in simplest form.

   Skill 5

   F $\frac{1}{2}$ H $\frac{5}{5}$

   G $\frac{7}{10}$ J $\frac{7}{5}$

5. Find $\frac{3}{8} + \frac{1}{8}$ in simplest form.

   Skill 2

   A $\frac{1}{4}$ C $\frac{1}{3}$

   B $\frac{1}{2}$ D $\frac{4}{16}$

6. In Mr. Sinclair's class, $\frac{5}{8}$ of the students have brown hair and $\frac{1}{4}$ have black hair. What fraction of the students have neither brown nor black hair?

   Skill 8

   F $\frac{1}{8}$ H $\frac{1}{2}$

   G $\frac{1}{4}$ J $\frac{7}{8}$

7. Which of he following is the best estimate of $6\frac{1}{8} - 3\frac{7}{9}$?

   Skill 1

   A 2   C 4

   B 3   D 9

8. Jesse walks $\frac{3}{8}$ of a mile to the park and then $\frac{1}{4}$ of a mile to his home. How far does he walk in all?

   Skill 3

   F $\frac{1}{2}$ mi   H $\frac{3}{4}$ mi

   G $\frac{2}{3}$ mi   J $\frac{5}{8}$ mi

9. Find $1\frac{3}{4} + 2\frac{1}{2}$ in simplest form.

   Skill 4

   A $3\frac{2}{3}$ C $4\frac{1}{5}$

   B $4\frac{1}{4}$ D $4\frac{3}{4}$

10. Find $6\frac{1}{4} - 1\frac{3}{4}$ in simplest form.

    Skill 6

    F $4\frac{1}{4}$ H $4\frac{1}{2}$

    G $5\frac{1}{4}$ J $5\frac{1}{2}$

11. Find $8\frac{1}{3} - 4\frac{3}{4}$ in simplest form.

    Skill 7

    A $3\frac{5}{12}$ C $4\frac{5}{12}$

    B $3\frac{7}{12}$ D $4\frac{7}{12}$

12. Wynn needs $2\frac{5}{6}$ feet of felt to make a banner and $1\frac{3}{8}$ feet of felt to make the designs. How much felt does he need in all?

    Skill 4

    F $3\frac{4}{7}$ ft   H $4\frac{9}{24}$ ft

    G $4\frac{5}{24}$ ft   J $4\frac{1}{3}$ ft

Mixed Review for Section A

What kind of poem does a poet write in outer space?

To find the answer to the riddle, first find the answer to each exercise. Write each answer in simplest form. At the bottom of the page, write the letter on the blank above the answer. Some answers are not used.

D **1.** $\frac{1}{6} + \frac{5}{8} =$ _____

M **2.** $\frac{9}{10} - \frac{3}{10} =$ _____

L **3.** $3\frac{1}{4} - 2\frac{1}{2} =$ _____

S **4.** $5 - 1\frac{1}{3} =$ _____

E **5.** $\frac{5}{9} + \frac{8}{9} =$ _____

R **6.** $\frac{11}{12} - \frac{5}{6} =$ _____

C **7.** $4\frac{3}{8} - 1\frac{5}{8} =$ _____

O **8.** $1\frac{2}{5} + 1\frac{3}{5} =$ _____

I **9.** $2\frac{3}{4} + 1\frac{7}{8} =$ _____

A **10.** $\frac{3}{10} + \frac{1}{6} =$ _____

H **11.** $3\frac{2}{3} - 2\frac{1}{6} =$ _____

N **12.** $3\frac{3}{4} + \frac{2}{3} =$ _____

U **13.** $\frac{3}{4} - \frac{7}{12} =$ _____

P **14.** $2 + 3\frac{1}{2} =$ _____

V **15.** $8\frac{1}{2} - 5\frac{1}{3} =$ _____

E **16.** $3\frac{1}{2} + 2\frac{5}{6} =$ _____

___ ___ ___ ___ - ___ ___ ___ ___ ___ ___

$\frac{7}{15}$ $\frac{1}{6}$ $4\frac{5}{12}$ $4\frac{5}{8}$ $3\frac{1}{6}$ $1\frac{4}{9}$ $\frac{1}{12}$ $3\frac{2}{3}$ $6\frac{1}{3}$

SKILL 9: Estimating Products

You can round to estimate products of fractions and mixed numbers.

- Round each factor to the nearest whole number.
- Multiply the whole numbers.

Example

Estimate: $4\frac{3}{5} \times 2\frac{3}{8}$.

Compare the fractions to $\frac{1}{2}$.	Round each fraction to either 0 or 1.	Add the rounded fraction to the whole number.	Multiply.
$\frac{3}{5} \geq \frac{1}{2}$	$\frac{3}{5}$ rounds to 1.	$4 + 1 = 5$	$5 \times 2 = 10$
$\frac{3}{8} < \frac{1}{2}$	$\frac{3}{8}$ rounds to 0.	$2 + 0 = 2$	

So, $4\frac{3}{5} \times 2\frac{3}{8}$ is about 10.

Guided Practice

1. Estimate: $2\frac{2}{3} \times 5\frac{4}{9}$.

    a. Round each fraction to either 0 or 1. $\frac{2}{3} \rightarrow$ ____ $\frac{4}{9} \rightarrow$ ____

    b. Round each mixed number: $2\frac{2}{3} \rightarrow 2 +$ ____ $=$ ____

                         $5\frac{4}{9} \rightarrow 5 +$ ____ $=$ ____

    c. Multiply to obtain the estimated product. ____ $\times$ ____ $=$ ____

2. Estimate: $\frac{1}{8} \times 1\frac{5}{6}$.

    a. Round to the nearest whole number: $\frac{1}{8} \rightarrow$ ____ $1\frac{5}{6} \rightarrow$ ____

    b. Multiply to obtain the estimated product. ____ $\times$ ____ $=$ ____

Estimate each product. Show your rounded factors.

3. $3\frac{7}{9} \times 5\frac{4}{15} \rightarrow$ ____ $\times$ ____ $=$ ____   **4.** $8\frac{4}{9} \times 6\frac{5}{8} \rightarrow$ ____ $\times$ ____ $=$ ____

5. $1\frac{1}{4} \times 2\frac{7}{8} \rightarrow$ ____ $\times$ ____ $=$ ____   **6.** $\frac{4}{5} \times 1\frac{1}{3} \rightarrow$ ____ $\times$ ____ $=$ ____

7. $3\frac{5}{6} \times 4\frac{2}{3} \rightarrow$ ____ $\times$ ____ $=$ ____   **8.** $\frac{2}{3} \times \frac{3}{4} \rightarrow$ ____ $\times$ ____ $=$ ____

9. $8\frac{1}{2} \times 6\frac{1}{4} \rightarrow$ ____ $\times$ ____ $=$ ____   **10.** $\frac{8}{9} \times 1\frac{1}{10} \rightarrow$ ____ $\times$ ____ $=$ ____

11. $5\frac{1}{3} \times \frac{3}{4} \rightarrow$ ____ $\times$ ____ $=$ ____   **12.** $\frac{3}{8} \times \frac{1}{5} \rightarrow$ ____ $\times$ ____ $=$ ____

SKILL 9: Practice

Estimate each product.

1. $6\frac{1}{3} \times 12\frac{1}{7}$ _____

2. $7\frac{9}{10} \times 3\frac{1}{3}$ _____

3. $4\frac{2}{3} \times 3\frac{3}{4}$ _____

4. $\frac{2}{5} \times \frac{2}{3}$ _____

5. $3\frac{1}{3} \times 5\frac{1}{7}$ _____

6. $\frac{3}{5} \times 7\frac{1}{5}$ _____

7. $7\frac{5}{8} \times 9\frac{3}{5}$ _____

8. $\frac{2}{9} \times \frac{3}{5}$ _____

9. $7\frac{1}{4} \times 13\frac{4}{5}$ _____

10. $9\frac{1}{4} \times \frac{3}{4}$ _____

11. $2\frac{1}{2} \times 3\frac{4}{9}$ _____

12. $\frac{7}{8} \times 3\frac{2}{9}$ _____

13. $4\frac{4}{5} \times 5\frac{1}{2}$ _____

14. $\frac{2}{3} \times 4\frac{1}{3}$ _____

15. $7\frac{2}{5} \times 7\frac{1}{2}$ _____

16. $\frac{5}{7} \times \frac{2}{3}$ _____

17. $\frac{3}{7} \times \frac{1}{6}$ _____

18. $7\frac{2}{3} \times 6\frac{1}{3}$ _____

19. $8\frac{2}{3} \times 9\frac{8}{9}$ _____

20. $1\frac{3}{8} \times 5\frac{2}{5}$ _____

21. $4\frac{2}{5} \times 6\frac{1}{2}$ _____

22. $8\frac{3}{5} \times 4\frac{1}{10}$ _____

23. $3\frac{3}{4} \times 3\frac{7}{10}$ _____

24. $2\frac{3}{4} \times 7\frac{1}{2}$ _____

25. $9\frac{4}{7} \times 12\frac{5}{7}$ _____

26. $9\frac{2}{5} \times 4\frac{1}{3}$ _____

27. $8\frac{7}{9} \times 9\frac{4}{9}$ _____

Solve.

28. A CD case measures $5\frac{5}{8}$ inches across. A music store manager wants to display 7 CDs side-by-side on a 42-inch shelf. Is there enough room for the display? _____

29. A lasagna recipe calls for $1\frac{1}{4}$ pounds of mozzarella cheese. About how much cheese should Tanya buy to make $2\frac{1}{2}$ times the recipe? _____

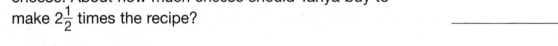

TEST PREP

30. Which is the best estimate of $5\frac{3}{4} \times 2\frac{1}{5}$?

Skill 9

A 8   **C** 12

B 10   **D** 18

31. Bryce has $\frac{5}{6}$ yard of ribbon. He uses $\frac{1}{6}$ yard to wrap a gift. How much ribbon does he have left?

Skill 5

F $\frac{1}{6}$ yd   **H** $\frac{4}{5}$ yd

G $\frac{2}{3}$ yd   **J** $1\frac{1}{6}$ yd

SKILL 10: Multiplying Fractions

You can use a diagram to help you multiply a fraction by a fraction.

Example 1

Multiply: $\frac{1}{2} \times \frac{3}{4}$.

Draw a diagram to show $\frac{3}{4}$.

Now shade $\frac{1}{2}$ of the rectangle.

The area where the shaded regions overlap shows $\frac{1}{2}$ of $\frac{3}{4}$.

So, $\frac{1}{2} \times \frac{3}{4} = \frac{3}{8}$.

To multiply two fractions, write the product of the numerators over the product of the denominators. Check that your answer is in simplest form.

Example 2

Find $\frac{3}{8} \times \frac{2}{3}$ in simplest form.

$\frac{3}{8} \times \frac{2}{3} = \frac{3 \times 2}{8 \times 3}$ Multiply the numerators
Multiply the denominators.

$= \frac{6}{24}$ Simplify.

$= \frac{1}{4}$

So, $\frac{3}{8} \times \frac{2}{3} = \frac{1}{4}$.

Guided Practice

Find each product in simplest form. You may use a diagram if you like.

1. $\frac{1}{2} \times \frac{5}{6} =$ _____

2. $\frac{4}{5} \times \frac{2}{3} = \frac{\Box \times \Box}{\Box \times \Box} =$ _____

3. $\frac{5}{8} \times \frac{1}{2} = \frac{\Box \times \Box}{\Box \times \Box} =$ _____

4. $\frac{3}{7} \times \frac{1}{6} = \frac{\Box \times \Box}{\Box \times \Box} =$ _____

5. $\frac{3}{4} \times \frac{8}{9} = \frac{\Box \times \Box}{\Box \times \Box} =$ _____

SKILL 10: Practice

Find each product in simplest form.

1. $\frac{1}{2} \times \frac{1}{2} =$ _____

2. $\frac{2}{3} \times \frac{9}{10} =$ _____

3. $\frac{1}{4} \times \frac{3}{5} =$ _____

4. $\frac{1}{4} \times \frac{1}{2} =$ _____

5. $\frac{5}{6} \times \frac{2}{3} =$ _____

6. $\frac{5}{8} \times \frac{1}{9} =$ _____

7. $\frac{1}{7} \times \frac{1}{2} =$ _____

8. $\frac{2}{3} \times \frac{4}{9} =$ _____

9. $\frac{5}{8} \times \frac{3}{8} =$ _____

10. $\frac{1}{2} \times \frac{4}{13} =$ _____

11. $\frac{1}{3} \times \frac{2}{7} =$ _____

12. $\frac{13}{15} \times \frac{1}{4} =$ _____

13. $\frac{2}{5} \times \frac{4}{5} =$ _____

14. $\frac{1}{11} \times \frac{2}{5} =$ _____

15. $\frac{7}{9} \times \frac{2}{11} =$ _____

16. $\frac{3}{4} \times \frac{1}{2} =$ _____

17. $\frac{1}{2} \times \frac{14}{15} =$ _____

18. $\frac{1}{5} \times \frac{1}{3} =$ _____

19. $\frac{11}{15} \times \frac{1}{10} =$ _____

20. $\frac{8}{9} \times \frac{2}{7} =$ _____

21. $\frac{7}{8} \times \frac{11}{14} =$ _____

22. $\frac{1}{2} \times \frac{5}{7} =$ _____

23. $\frac{3}{4} \times \frac{1}{3} =$ _____

24. $\frac{1}{2} \times \frac{7}{8} =$ _____

25. $\frac{12}{13} \times \frac{3}{10} =$ _____

26. $\frac{2}{3} \times \frac{1}{3} =$ _____

27. $\frac{2}{3} \times \frac{7}{9} =$ _____

Solve.

28. The total weight of all of the insects in the world is about $\frac{7}{20}$ billion tons. The total weight of all humans is about $\frac{1}{3}$ of this amount. Find the total weight of all humans.

_____

29. A recipe for granola bars calls for $\frac{2}{3}$ cup of oats. How much of the oats would you use to make $\frac{1}{2}$ of the amount in the original recipe?

_____

30. Multiply: $\frac{8}{9} \times \frac{3}{10}$.   *Skill 10*

    A $\frac{2}{9}$ **C** $\frac{11}{90}$

    B $\frac{4}{15}$ **D** $\frac{27}{80}$

31. Which is the best estimate of $1\frac{8}{9} \times 2\frac{6}{7}$?   *Skill 9*

    F 2   **H** 6

    G 4   **J** 8

SKILL 11: Multiplying a Fraction by a Whole Number

To multiply a fraction by a whole number, first write the whole number as an improper fraction. Then write the product of the numerators over the product of the denominators. Simplify if necessary.

Example

Multiply: $6 \times \frac{3}{4}$.

Write the whole number as an improper fraction.

$$6 \times \frac{3}{4} - \frac{6}{1} \times \frac{3}{4}$$

Multiply the numerators. Then multiply the denominators.

$$= \frac{6 \times 3}{1 \times 4}$$

Multiply and simplify.

$$= \frac{18}{4} = 4\frac{2}{4} = 4\frac{1}{2}$$

So, $6 \times \frac{3}{4} = 4\frac{1}{2}$.

Guided Practice

1. Multiply: $\frac{2}{3} \times 5$.

   a. Write the whole number as an improper fraction.

   b. Multiply numerators and denominators.

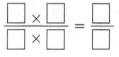

   c. Simplify.

Multiply. Simplify each product.

2. $\frac{3}{8} \times 9 = \frac{3}{8} \times \frac{\square}{\square} = \frac{\square \times \square}{\square \times \square} = $ _____

3. $\frac{1}{2} \times 8 = \frac{1}{2} \times \frac{\square}{\square} = \frac{\square \times \square}{\square \times \square} = $ _____

4. $12 \times \frac{4}{5} = \frac{\square}{1} \times \frac{\square}{\square} = \frac{\square \times \square}{\square \times \square} = $ _____

5. $2 \times \frac{5}{6} = $ _____

6. $9 \times \frac{2}{3} = $ _____

7. $8 \times \frac{3}{5} = $ _____

8. $\frac{5}{8} \times 9 = $ _____

9. $5 \times \frac{2}{7} = $ _____

10. $7 \times \frac{3}{4} = $ _____

SKILL 11: Practice

Multiply. Simplify each product.

1. $10 \times \frac{3}{8} =$ _____

2. $12 \times \frac{1}{2} =$ _____

3. $4 \times \frac{2}{5} =$ _____

4. $\frac{4}{5} \times 15 =$ _____

5. $3 \times \frac{11}{12} =$ _____

6. $7 \times \frac{4}{5} =$ _____

7. $\frac{2}{7} \times 6 =$ _____

8. $\frac{2}{3} \times 9 =$ _____

9. $\frac{7}{10} \times 5 =$ _____

10. $9 \times \frac{5}{6} =$ _____

11. $8 \times \frac{2}{3} =$ _____

12. $\frac{1}{4} \times 16 =$ _____

13. $12 \times \frac{3}{8} =$ _____

14. $\frac{3}{4} \times 6 =$ _____

15. $\frac{3}{8} \times 8 =$ _____

16. $\frac{2}{3} \times 12 =$ _____

17. $2 \times \frac{5}{12} =$ _____

18. $4 \times \frac{5}{8} =$ _____

19. $3 \times \frac{8}{9} =$ _____

20. $\frac{3}{10} \times 5 =$ _____

21. $8 \times \frac{5}{12} =$ _____

22. $\frac{1}{6} \times 9 =$ _____

23. $6 \times \frac{4}{6} =$ _____

24. $12 \times \frac{5}{8} =$ _____

Solve.

25. Amal's bones make up about $\frac{1}{5}$ of his body weight. He weighs 140 pounds. How many pounds do his bones weigh? _____

26. Jessica bought a 5-gallon can of paint. After painting her room, $\frac{2}{5}$ of the paint was left. How many gallons of paint did she use? _____

27. What is $2 \times \frac{7}{10}$?

Skill 11

A $\frac{9}{10}$

C $1\frac{4}{5}$

B $1\frac{2}{5}$

D $2\frac{7}{10}$

28. Find $8\frac{1}{4} + 3\frac{7}{8}$ in lowest terms.

Skill 4

F $11\frac{1}{8}$

H $12\frac{1}{8}$

G $1\frac{2}{3}$

J $12\frac{8}{9}$

Section B: Multiplying Fractions

SKILL 12: Multiplying Mixed Numbers

To multiply two mixed numbers, first write each mixed number
as an improper fraction. Then multiply the two improper fractions.
Be sure to write the product in simplest form.

Example 1

Multiply: $1\frac{1}{2} \times 3\frac{1}{2}$.

Write each mixed number as an improper fraction. $1\frac{1}{2} \times 3\frac{1}{2} = \frac{3}{2} \times \frac{7}{2}$

Multiply the numerators.
Then multiply the denominators. $= \frac{3 \times 7}{2 \times 2}$

Multiply and simplify. $= \frac{21}{4} = 5\frac{1}{4}$

So, $1\frac{1}{2} \times 3\frac{1}{2} = 5\frac{1}{4}$.

Example 2

Multiply: $4 \times 1\frac{3}{5}$.

Write each factor as an improper fraction. $4 \times 1\frac{3}{5} = \frac{4}{1} \times \frac{8}{5}$

Multiply the numerators.
Then multiply the denominators. $= \frac{4 \times 8}{1 \times 5}$

Multiply and simplify. $= \frac{32}{5} = 6\frac{2}{5}$

So, $4 \times 1\frac{3}{5} = 6\frac{2}{5}$.

Guided Practice

1. Multiply: $\frac{7}{8} \times 1\frac{1}{4}$.

    a. Write the mixed number $1\frac{1}{4} = \frac{\Box}{\Box}$
        as an improper fraction.

    b. Multiply numerators and denominators. $\frac{\Box \times \Box}{\Box \times \Box} = \frac{\Box}{\Box}$

    c. Simplify. _____.

2. Multiply: $1\frac{3}{4} \times 2\frac{1}{2}$.

    a. Write each mixed numbers $1\frac{3}{4} = \frac{\Box}{\Box}$; $2\frac{1}{2} = \frac{\Box}{\Box}$
        as an improper fraction.

    b. Multiply and simplify.   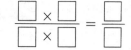 _____

SKILL 12: Practice

Multiply. Simplify each product.

1. $3\frac{3}{4} \times 2\frac{1}{2} =$ _____

2. $1\frac{3}{8} \times 2\frac{1}{4} =$ _____

3. $5 \times 2\frac{1}{8} =$ _____

4. $3\frac{2}{3} \times 1\frac{1}{2} =$ _____

5. $\frac{1}{3} \times 2\frac{5}{6} =$ _____

6. $2\frac{1}{5} \times 1\frac{5}{6} =$ _____

7. $3\frac{1}{4} \times 2\frac{2}{3} =$ _____

8. $2 \times 1\frac{3}{10} =$ _____

9. $1\frac{2}{5} \times 3\frac{1}{3} =$ _____

10. $1\frac{1}{6} \times 3\frac{1}{5} =$ _____

11. $4 \times 3\frac{1}{3} =$ _____

12. $6\frac{1}{2} \times 1\frac{3}{5} =$ _____

13. $4\frac{1}{2} \times 1\frac{1}{4} =$ _____

14. $1\frac{3}{4} \times 5 =$ _____

15. $1\frac{1}{8} \times 2\frac{1}{6} =$ _____

16. $3 \times 3\frac{1}{6} =$ _____

17. $1\frac{1}{4} \times 5\frac{1}{3} =$ _____

18. $2\frac{2}{5} \times 1\frac{1}{2} =$ _____

19. $4\frac{2}{3} \times 1\frac{1}{8} =$ _____

20. $3\frac{3}{4} \times 4\frac{1}{5} =$ _____

21. $\frac{2}{3} \times 2\frac{1}{2} =$ _____

22. $2\frac{1}{4} \times 5\frac{2}{3} =$ _____

23. $2\frac{2}{3} \times 6\frac{1}{2} =$ _____

24. $1\frac{1}{8} \times 6 =$ _____

Solve.

25. A certain granola cereal has 240 calories in each 1 cup serving. How many calories are in a serving of $1\frac{1}{3}$ cups of the cereal? _____

26. Samantha earns $18 per hour. How much will she earn if she works for $12\frac{3}{4}$ hours? _____

27. Find the product: $2\frac{1}{2} \times 3\frac{1}{5}$.

    Skill 12

    A $2\frac{1}{10}$ **C** $6\frac{1}{10}$

    B $6\frac{1}{7}$ **D** 8

28. Which is the best estimate of $1\frac{3}{10} \times 5\frac{1}{9}$?

    Skill 9

    F 0   **H** 10

    G 5   **J** 12

Section B: Multiplying Fractions

SKILL 13: PROBLEM SOLVING: Overestimating and Underestimating

Sometimes you must overestimate or underestimate to find a useful solution to a problem. To overestimate a product, round the factors so the estimate is greater than the exact product. To underestimate a product, round the factors so the estimate is less than the exact product.

Example

Each student in Mr. Ruiz's class needs $3\frac{3}{8}$ pounds of clay for an art project. There are 12 students in his class. How much clay should he order for the project?

Read Mr. Ruiz needs enough clay so each student has $3\frac{3}{8}$ pounds. There are 12 students.

Plan Overestimate to make sure that Mr. Ruiz will have enough clay.

Solve Overestimate the product of $3\frac{3}{8} \times 12$.

Round the mixed number, $3\frac{3}{8}$ to the next greater whole number, 4.

Estimate the product: $4 \times 12 = 48$. He needs about 48 pounds of clay.

Look Back Why does overestimation make sense in this case? Overestimation means that he will have enough for all the students.

Guided Practice

Josh earns $12 per hour. He worked $8\frac{1}{2}$ hours last week. He was hoping to work enough hours to be able to buy new speakers that cost $105. Use an estimate to decide if he earned enough money.

1. Should you overestimate or underestimate? Why?

_____

2. Estimate the product. _____

3. Do you think that he earned enough money? _____

4. About how many hours should he have worked? Why? _____

_____

SKILL 13: Practice

Overestimate or underestimate to solve each problem.
Explain why you chose to overestimate or underestimate.

1. A carpenter needs $2\frac{7}{8}$ feet of wood for each shelf in a bookcase he is building. About how many feet of wood will he need to make 8 shelves?

_____

2. Sarah is training for a race. She wants to run at least 12 miles a week to prepare for the race. If she runs $3\frac{1}{4}$ miles each day for 5 days, will she meet her goal?

_____

3. A painter needs $15\frac{1}{3}$ feet of wire to hang each painting in an exhibit. She has 8 paintings to hang. Will 120 feet of wire be enough for her to hang all of the paintings?

_____

4. Alyssa earns $12 for each hour that she does yard work. She wants to earn enough money to buy a pair of concert tickets that cost a total of $75. She has already worked for $5\frac{3}{4}$ hours. Has she earned enough money to buy the tickets yet?

_____

5. Devin has 3 hours to finish his homework and his chores before he can go to the movies. If he spends $1\frac{3}{4}$ hours doing his homework and $\frac{5}{6}$ hours completing his chores, will he be finished in time to go to the movies?

_____

6. Jack is making fruit punch for a party. He has invited 9 people and expects each person to drink $3\frac{1}{2}$ cups. How many cups should he make to be sure to have enough?

Skill 13

A 36   C 27
B 30   D 45

7. Delia has 3 cups of milk. She uses $\frac{3}{4}$ cup milk in one recipe and $1\frac{2}{3}$ cups milk in another recipe. How much milk does she have left?

Skill 8

F $\frac{5}{12}$ c   H $1\frac{5}{12}$ c
G $\frac{7}{12}$ c   J $2\frac{5}{12}$ c

© Prentice-Hall, Inc.

Circle each correct answer.

1. Find $\frac{2}{3} \times \frac{3}{4}$ in simplest form.

   Skill 10

   A $\frac{5}{12}$　　　**C** $\frac{7}{12}$

   B $\frac{1}{2}$　　　**D** $\frac{5}{7}$

2. Find $\frac{3}{8} \times 2$ in simplest form.

   Skill 11

   F $\frac{3}{4}$　　　**H** $\frac{5}{8}$

   G $\frac{3}{8}$　　　**J** $\frac{3}{16}$

3. Estimate: $6\frac{5}{6} \times 3\frac{1}{9}$.

   Skill 9

   A 10　　　**C** 21

   B 18　　　**D** 28

4. A painter had $4\frac{1}{2}$ gallons of paint. He needed $\frac{3}{4}$ of the paint to complete his painting. How much paint did he use to complete the painting?

   Skill 12

   F $1\frac{1}{2}$ gal　　　**H** $3\frac{3}{8}$ gal

   G $2\frac{3}{8}$ gal　　　**J** $4\frac{3}{8}$ gal

5. Manuel needs $1\frac{2}{3}$ cups of raisins to make one recipe of snack bars. About how many cups of raisins should he have on hand to have enough for 8 recipes?

   Skill 13

   A 8 c　　　**C** 16 c

   B 12 c　　　**D** 20 c

6. Find $3\frac{3}{4} \times 1\frac{3}{5}$ in simplest form.

   Skill 12

   F $3\frac{9}{20}$　　　**H** 6

   G $5\frac{3}{4}$　　　**J** 7

7. Last week Parker ran $5\frac{1}{4}$ miles. This week he ran $2\frac{1}{8}$ times as far as last week. Estimate the number of miles he ran this week.

   Skill 9

   A 7 mi　　　**C** 15 mi

   B 10 mi　　　**D** 18 mi

8. Maggie needs to make 6 tablecloths. She uses $3\frac{3}{5}$ yards of fabric for each tablecloth. Which is the shortest roll that will have enough fabric for Maggie to be able to make all of the tablecloths?

   Skill 13

   F 15 yd　　　**H** 24 yd

   G 18 yd　　　**J** 28 yd

9. What is $\frac{3}{4} \times \frac{8}{15}$ in simplest form?

   Skill 10

   A $\frac{1}{3}$　　　**C** $\frac{11}{19}$

   B $\frac{2}{5}$　　　**D** $\frac{11}{60}$

10. Tricia has 12 feet of nylon cord. She uses $\frac{5}{6}$ of the cord for her climbing equipment. How many feet of nylon cord does she use?

    Skill 11

    F $\frac{5}{72}$ ft　　　**H** 8 ft

    G $1\frac{2}{5}$ ft　　　**J** 10 ft

11. Estimate: $1\frac{1}{3} \times 4\frac{5}{8}$.

    Skill 9

    A 10　　　**C** 8

    B 5　　　**D** 4

Mixed Review for Section B

Fraction Frame-Up

Each frame holds a number.

[ ] holds the number $\frac{3}{10}$.

[ ] holds the number $1\frac{2}{3}$.

$\frac{3}{8}$	$1\frac{5}{6}$	$2\frac{1}{4}$
$\frac{3}{10}$	8	$1\frac{2}{3}$
$\frac{4}{9}$	$3\frac{1}{5}$	$4\frac{1}{2}$

Write the correct numbers in the frames below. Then find each product in simplest form.

1. $\boxed{\frac{3}{10}} \times \boxed{1\frac{2}{3}}$ = _____

2. [ ] × [ ] = _____

3. [ ] × [ ] = _____

4. [ ] × [ ] = _____

5. [ ] × [ ] = _____

6. [ ] × [ ] = _____

7. [ ] × [ ] = _____

8. [ ] × [ ] = _____

9. [ ] × [ ] = _____

10. [ ] × [ ] = _____

11. [ ] × [ ] = _____

12. [ ] × [ ] = _____

13. [ ] × [ ] = _____

14. [ ] × [ ] = _____

Name _____ Date _____ Class _____

 # SKILL 14: Estimating Quotients

You can round to estimate quotients of fractions and mixed numbers.

- Round each factor to the nearest whole number.
- Divide the whole numbers.

Example

Estimate: $9\frac{7}{16} \div 2\frac{2}{3}$.

Compare each fractions to $\frac{1}{2}$.	Round each fraction to either 0 or 1.	Add the rounded fraction to the whole number.	Divide.
$\frac{7}{16} < \frac{1}{2}$	$\frac{7}{16}$ rounds to 0.	$9 + 0 = 9$	$9 \div 3 = 3$
$\frac{2}{3} \geq \frac{1}{2}$	$\frac{2}{3}$ rounds to 1.	$2 + 1 = 3$	

So, $9\frac{7}{16} \div 2\frac{2}{3}$ is about 3.

Guided Practice

1. Estimate: $12\frac{3}{14} \div 3\frac{7}{8}$.

   a. Round each fraction to either 0 or 1. $\frac{3}{14} \rightarrow$ ____ $\frac{7}{8} \rightarrow$ ____

   b. Round each mixed number. $12\frac{3}{14} \rightarrow 12 +$ ____ $=$ ____

                                $3\frac{7}{8} \rightarrow 3 +$ ____ $=$ ____

   c. Divide.   ____ $\div$ ____ $=$ ____

2. Estimate: $1\frac{2}{3} \div \frac{3}{4}$. Estimate each quotient.

   a. Round to the nearest whole number. $1\frac{2}{3} \rightarrow$ ____; $\frac{3}{4} \rightarrow$ ____

   b. Divide.   ____ $\div$ ____ $=$ ____

Estimate each quotient. Show your rounded numbers.

3. $14\frac{7}{8} \div 5\frac{2}{5}$ ____ $\div$ ____ $=$ ____   **4.** $75\frac{5}{24} \div 24\frac{17}{30}$ ____ $\div$ ____ $=$ ____

5. $\frac{7}{8} \div \frac{5}{6}$ ____ $\div$ ____ $=$ ____   **6.** $1\frac{1}{4} \div \frac{9}{10}$ ____ $\div$ ____ $=$ ____

7. $2\frac{1}{4} \div \frac{7}{10}$ ____ $\div$ ____ $=$ ____   **8.** $\frac{7}{9} \div \frac{3}{4}$ ____ $\div$ ____ $=$ ____

9. $6\frac{4}{5} \div 1\frac{1}{3}$ ____ $\div$ ____ $=$ ____   **10.** $9\frac{1}{8} \div 2\frac{7}{9}$ ____ $\div$ ____ $=$ ____

11. $7\frac{11}{12} \div 3\frac{5}{6}$ ____ $\div$ ____ $=$ ____   **12.** $8\frac{1}{5} \div 1\frac{2}{3}$ ____ $\div$ ____ $=$ ____

© Prentice-Hall, Inc.

Section C: Dividing Fractions   Operations with Fractions **31**

SKILL 14: Practice

Estimate each quotient.

1. $6\frac{1}{3} \div 2\frac{1}{7}$ _____

2. $7\frac{9}{10} \div 3\frac{1}{3}$ _____

3. $4\frac{2}{3} \div \frac{3}{4}$ _____

4. $7\frac{2}{5} \div 2\frac{2}{3}$ _____

5. $3\frac{1}{3} \div 1$ _____

6. $12\frac{3}{5} \div 7\frac{1}{5}$ _____

7. $7\frac{5}{8} \div \frac{3}{5}$ _____

8. $8\frac{2}{9} \div 3\frac{3}{5}$ _____

9. $6\frac{1}{4} \div 1\frac{4}{5}$ _____

10. $9\frac{1}{4} \div 3\frac{3}{4}$ _____

11. $2\frac{1}{2} \div 3\frac{4}{9}$ _____

12. $8\frac{7}{8} \div 3\frac{2}{9}$ _____

13. $\frac{4}{5} \div \frac{1}{2}$ _____

14. $8\frac{2}{3} \div 4\frac{1}{3}$ _____

15. $7\frac{2}{5} \div \frac{1}{2}$ _____

16. $6\frac{1}{7} \div 2\frac{2}{5}$ _____

17. $9\frac{3}{4} \div 1\frac{5}{6}$ _____

18. $10\frac{1}{9} \div 5\frac{1}{6}$ _____

19. $11\frac{2}{3} \div 6\frac{3}{7}$ _____

20. $3\frac{7}{10} \div 1\frac{1}{8}$ _____

21. $12\frac{4}{5} \div 6\frac{1}{2}$ _____

22. $10\frac{4}{9} \div 5\frac{5}{6}$ _____

23. $11\frac{3}{4} \div 1\frac{5}{7}$ _____

24. $10\frac{1}{6} \div 6\frac{1}{3}$ _____

25. $8\frac{3}{5} \div 4\frac{1}{10}$ _____

26. $3\frac{3}{4} \div 3\frac{7}{10}$ _____

27. $13\frac{3}{4} \div 7\frac{1}{2}$ _____

28. There are $2\frac{1}{4}$ gallons of gasoline in a car's gas tank. The car can travel $20\frac{1}{2}$ miles on a gallon of gasoline.

    a. Can the car be driven 63 miles without stopping for more gasoline? _____

    b. Why or why not? _____

TEST PREP

29. Estimate: $10\frac{1}{3} \div 2\frac{2}{5}$.

Skill 14

    A 3   **C** 5

    B 4   **D** 7

30. Multiply: $2\frac{2}{5} \times 3\frac{1}{2}$.

Skill 12

    F $6\frac{1}{5}$ **H** $8\frac{2}{5}$

    G $6\frac{2}{5}$ **J** $8\frac{4}{5}$

SKILL 15: Dividing a Whole Number by a Fraction

To do division such as $3 \div \frac{3}{4}$, you can think about how many $\frac{3}{4}$-inch strips can be placed along a 3-inch ruler.

Example 1

Divide: $3 \div \frac{3}{4}$.

You can see that there are $1\frac{1}{3}$ strips in 1 inch.

So, there are $3 \times 1\frac{1}{3}$ strips in 3 inches.

$$So, 3 \div \frac{3}{4} = 3 \times 1\frac{1}{3}$$
$$= \frac{3}{1} \times \frac{4}{3}$$
$$= \frac{12}{3}$$
$$= 4$$

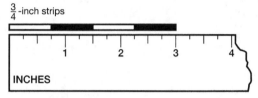

$\frac{3}{4}$-inch strips

INCHES

The model shows that $3 \div \frac{3}{4} = 4$.

Two numbers are **reciprocals** if their product is 1. In Example 1, $\frac{3}{4}$ and $\frac{4}{3}$ are reciprocals. Notice that dividing by a fraction gives the same result as multiplying by its reciprocal.

Example 2

Divide: $4 \div \frac{3}{8}$.

$$4 \div \frac{3}{8} = 4 \times \frac{8}{3} \qquad \text{Write the reciprocal of } \frac{3}{8} \text{ and}$$
change division to multiplication.

$$= \frac{4}{1} \times \frac{8}{3} \qquad \text{Write the whole number as an improper fraction.}$$

$$= \frac{4 \times 8}{1 \times 3} \qquad \text{Multiply.}$$

$$= \frac{32}{3}$$

$$= 10\frac{2}{3} \qquad \text{Write your answer in simplest form.}$$

So, $4 \div \frac{3}{8} = 10\frac{2}{3}$.

Guided Practice

Find each quotient in simplest form.

1. $10 \div \frac{1}{3}$

   a. The reciprocal of $\frac{1}{3}$ is $\frac{\square}{\square}$.

   b. $10 \div \frac{1}{3} = \frac{\square}{\square} \times \frac{\square}{\square} = \underline{\hspace{1cm}}$

2. $21 \div \frac{3}{5}$

   a. The reciprocal of $\frac{3}{5}$ is $\frac{\square}{\square}$.

   b. $21 \div \frac{3}{5} = \frac{\square}{1} \times \frac{\square}{\square} = \frac{\square}{\square} = \underline{\hspace{1cm}}$

SKILL 15: Practice

Write the reciprocal of each number.

1. $\frac{2}{3}$ = _____

2. $\frac{1}{8}$ = _____

3. $\frac{4}{7}$ = _____

4. $2\frac{1}{2}$ = _____

5. $\frac{1}{4}$ = _____

6. 5 = _____

Divide. Simplify each quotient.

7. $11 \div \frac{1}{7}$ = _____

8. $6 \div \frac{1}{3}$ = _____

9. $3 \div \frac{5}{8}$ = _____

10. $7 \div \frac{2}{3}$ = _____

11. $4 \div \frac{3}{4}$ = _____

12. $11 \div \frac{3}{4}$ = _____

13. $5 \div \frac{2}{9}$ = _____

14. $7 \div \frac{8}{9}$ = _____

15. $8 \div \frac{1}{3}$ = _____

16. $10 \div \frac{2}{9}$ = _____

17. $6 \div \frac{1}{2}$ = _____

18. $7 \div \frac{2}{9}$ = _____

19. $12 \div \frac{1}{3}$ = _____

20. $8 \div \frac{3}{7}$ = _____

21. $5 \div \frac{2}{5}$ = _____

22. $8 \div \frac{1}{7}$ = _____

23. $8 \div \frac{1}{3}$ = _____

24. $5 \div \frac{2}{3}$ = _____

25. $3 \div \frac{1}{3}$ = _____

26. $6 \div \frac{1}{5}$ = _____

27. $4 \div \frac{2}{5}$ = _____

Solve.

28. A baby walrus is 4 feet long. This is $\frac{2}{5}$ of the length of an adult male. What is the length of an adult male walrus? _____

29. One yard (36 inches) is equal to $\frac{2}{11}$ of a rod. How many inches are in a rod? _____

30. Divide: $10 \div \frac{4}{5}$.

Skill 15

    A $\frac{1}{8}$ **C** 8

    B $\frac{2}{25}$ **D** $12\frac{1}{2}$

31. Find $2\frac{2}{3} + 3\frac{2}{5}$ in simplest form.

Skill 4

    F $5\frac{1}{15}$ **H** $5\frac{1}{2}$

    G $5\frac{4}{15}$ **J** $6\frac{1}{15}$

SKILL 16: Dividing Fractions

To divide by a fraction, write the reciprocal of the divisor and change the division to multiplication.

Example

Find $\frac{5}{6} \div \frac{7}{8}$ in simplest form.

$\frac{5}{6} \div \frac{7}{8} = \frac{5}{6} \times \frac{8}{7}$ Write the reciprocal of the divisor and change the division to multiplication.

$= \frac{5 \times 8}{6 \times 7}$ Multiply.

$= \frac{40}{42}$ Check that your answer is in simplest form.

$= \frac{20}{21}$

So, $\frac{5}{6} \div \frac{7}{8} = \frac{20}{21}$.

Guided Practice

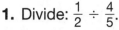

Divide. Write each quotient in simplest form.

1. Divide: $\frac{1}{2} \div \frac{4}{5}$.

     a. The reciprocal of $\frac{4}{5}$ is _____.

     b. Multiply by the reciprocal. $\frac{\square}{\square} \times \frac{\square}{\square} = $ _____

2. Divide: $\frac{3}{4} \div \frac{5}{12}$.

     a. The reciprocal of $\frac{5}{12}$ is _____.

     b. Multiply by the reciprocal. $\frac{\square}{\square} \times \frac{\square}{\square} = $ _____

     c. Simplify. _____

3. $\frac{5}{8} \div \frac{15}{16} = \frac{\square}{\square} \times \frac{\square}{\square} = $ _____

4. $\frac{3}{8} \div \frac{1}{2} = \frac{\square}{\square} \times \frac{\square}{\square} = $ _____

5. $\frac{7}{10} \div \frac{1}{6} = \frac{\square}{\square} \times \frac{\square}{\square} = $ _____

6. $\frac{8}{15} \div \frac{8}{9} = \frac{\square}{\square} \times \frac{\square}{\square} = $ _____

7. $\frac{4}{5} \div \frac{2}{3} = $ _____

8. $\frac{3}{8} \div \frac{3}{4} = $ _____

SKILL 16: Practice

Divide. Write each quotient in simplest form.

1. $\frac{1}{2} \div \frac{7}{10} =$ _____

2. $\frac{5}{12} \div \frac{1}{6} =$ _____

3. $\frac{4}{7} \div \frac{2}{3} =$ _____

4. $\frac{5}{6} \div \frac{1}{4} =$ _____

5. $\frac{9}{11} \div \frac{3}{7} =$ _____

6. $\frac{3}{4} \div \frac{5}{8} =$ _____

7. $\frac{1}{6} \div \frac{5}{8} =$ _____

8. $\frac{3}{4} \div \frac{1}{6} =$ _____

9. $\frac{11}{12} \div \frac{1}{4} =$ _____

10. $\frac{3}{4} \div \frac{5}{12} =$ _____

11. $\frac{7}{12} \div \frac{2}{3} =$ _____

12. $\frac{5}{8} \div \frac{1}{6} =$ _____

13. $\frac{5}{6} \div \frac{3}{10} =$ _____

14. $\frac{2}{5} \div \frac{3}{10} =$ _____

15. $\frac{4}{5} \div \frac{2}{7} =$ _____

16. $\frac{2}{3} \div \frac{4}{9} =$ _____

17. $\frac{5}{9} \div \frac{1}{3} =$ _____

18. $\frac{1}{4} \div \frac{7}{8} =$ _____

Solve.

19. A soup recipe calls for $\frac{3}{8}$ of a cup of olive oil.
One tablespoon is equal to $\frac{1}{16}$ of a cup. How many
tablespoons of olive oil are needed to make the soup?   _____

20. A sheet of posterboard is $\frac{1}{24}$ in. thick. How many
sheets of this posterboard are needed to make a
stack $\frac{3}{4}$ in. high?   _____

21. Divide: $\frac{5}{9} \div \frac{2}{3}$.   *Skill 16*

    A $\frac{3}{5}$ **C** $\frac{10}{27}$

    B $\frac{5}{6}$ **D** $1\frac{1}{5}$

22. Which is the best estimate
of $5\frac{6}{7} + 3\frac{7}{12}$?   *Skill 1*

    F 8   **H** 10

    G 9   **J** 11

SKILL 17: Dividing a Fraction by a Whole Number

To divide a fraction by a whole number, write the whole number
as an improper fraction. Then divide the fractions.

Example

Find $\frac{5}{6} \div 3$ in simplest form.

$\frac{5}{6} \div 3 = \frac{5}{6} \div \frac{3}{1}$ Write the whole number as an improper fraction.

$\quad\quad = \frac{5}{6} \times \frac{1}{3}$ Write the reciprocal of the divisor and change
the division to multiplication.

$\quad\quad = \frac{5 \times 1}{6 \times 3}$ Multiply.

$\quad\quad = \frac{5}{18}$ Check that your answer is in simplest form.

So, $\frac{5}{6} \div 3 = \frac{5}{18}$.

Guided Practice

Find each quotient in simplest form.

1. Divide: $\frac{3}{4} \div 9$.

   a. 9 as an improper fraction is $\frac{\square}{\square}$.

   b. The reciprocal of 9 is $\frac{\square}{\square}$.

   c. $\frac{3}{4} \div 9 = \frac{\square}{\square} \times \frac{\square}{\square} = $ _____

2. Divide: $\frac{3}{8} \div 4$.

   a. 4 as an improper fraction is $\frac{\square}{\square}$.

   b. The reciprocal of 4 is $\frac{\square}{\square}$.

   c. $\frac{3}{8} \div 4 = \frac{\square}{\square} \times \frac{\square}{\square} = $ _____

3. Divide: $\frac{4}{5} \div 6$.

   a. 6 as an improper fraction is $\frac{\square}{\square}$.

   b. The reciprocal of 6 is $\frac{\square}{\square}$.

   c. $\frac{4}{5} \div 6 = \frac{\square}{\square} \times \frac{\square}{\square} = $ _____

4. Divide: $\frac{5}{7} \div 3$.

   a. 3 as an improper fraction is $\frac{\square}{\square}$.

   b. The reciprocal of 3 is $\frac{\square}{\square}$.

   c. $\frac{5}{7} \div 3 = \frac{\square}{\square} \times \frac{\square}{\square} = $ _____

5. $\frac{1}{5} \div 3 = \frac{\square}{\square} \times \frac{\square}{\square} = $ _____

6. $\frac{3}{4} \div 2 = \frac{\square}{\square} \times \frac{\square}{\square} = $ _____

7. $\frac{2}{3} \div 9 = \frac{\square}{\square} \times \frac{\square}{\square} = $ _____

8. $\frac{2}{5} \div 4 = \frac{\square}{\square} \times \frac{\square}{\square} = $ _____

SKILL 17: Practice

Divide. Simplify each quotient.

1. $\frac{3}{5} \div 5 =$ _____

2. $\frac{2}{7} \div 4 =$ _____

3. $\frac{9}{11} \div 3 =$ _____

4. $\frac{2}{3} \div 10 =$ _____

5. $\frac{3}{4} \div 12 =$ _____

6. $\frac{4}{5} \div 10 =$ _____

7. $\frac{1}{6} \div 3 =$ _____

8. $\frac{3}{5} \div 2 =$ _____

9. $\frac{6}{11} \div 4 =$ _____

10. $\frac{3}{5} \div 4 =$ _____

11. $\frac{5}{9} \div 10 =$ _____

12. $\frac{3}{8} \div 6 =$ _____

13. $\frac{3}{8} \div 9 =$ _____

14. $\frac{5}{6} \div 2 =$ _____

15. $\frac{3}{4} \div 4 =$ _____

16. $\frac{3}{10} \div 6 =$ _____

17. $\frac{4}{11} \div 6 =$ _____

18. $\frac{4}{5} \div 8 =$ _____

19. $\frac{5}{12} \div 10 =$ _____

20. $\frac{6}{7} \div 9 =$ _____

21. $\frac{6}{7} \div 3 =$ _____

22. $\frac{2}{3} \div 5 =$ _____

23. $\frac{5}{6} \div 3 =$ _____

24. $\frac{5}{8} \div 2 =$ _____

Solve.

25. A carpenter cuts a board that is $\frac{3}{4}$ meter long into 6 pieces of equal length. How long is each piece? _____

26. Toni wants to store $\frac{1}{2}$ gallon of sauce in 5 containers. If she wants each container to have the same amount of sauce, how much should she put in each container? _____

27. Find $\frac{6}{7} \div 8$ in simplest form.

Skill 17

A $\frac{1}{9}$ **C** $\frac{7}{28}$

B $\frac{3}{28}$ **D** $6\frac{6}{7}$

28. Find $4\frac{1}{3} \times 1\frac{1}{2}$ in simplest form.

Skill 12

F $4\frac{1}{6}$ **H** $5\frac{1}{5}$

G $4\frac{1}{3}$ **J** $6\frac{1}{2}$

SKILL 18: Dividing Mixed Numbers

To divide mixed numbers, write each mixed number as an improper fraction. Then divide.

Example 1

Find the reciprocal of $3\frac{4}{5}$.

The mixed number $3\frac{4}{5}$ has the same reciprocal as the improper fraction $\frac{19}{5}$.

Write the reciprocal.

So, the reciprocal of $3\frac{4}{5}$ is $\frac{5}{19}$.

$3\frac{4}{5} = \frac{19}{5}$

Since $\frac{19}{5} \times \frac{5}{19} = 1$, the reciprocal of $\frac{19}{5}$ is $\frac{5}{19}$.

Example 2

Divide: $3\frac{2}{3} \div 1\frac{3}{4}$.

$$3\frac{2}{3} \div 1\frac{3}{4} = \frac{11}{3} \div \frac{7}{4}$$ Write the mixed numbers as improper fractions.

$$= \frac{11}{3} \times \frac{4}{7}$$ Write the reciprocal of the divisor and change the division to multiplication.

$$= \frac{11 \times 4}{3 \times 7}$$ Multiply.

$$= \frac{44}{21}$$ Check that your answer is in simplest form.

$$= 2\frac{2}{21}$$

So, $3\frac{2}{3} \div 1\frac{3}{4} = 2\frac{2}{21}$.

Guided Practice

Write each mixed number as an improper fraction and find its reciprocal.

1. $3\frac{1}{2} = \frac{\square}{2}$.   Reciprocal: $\frac{\square}{\square}$.

2. $2\frac{3}{4} = \frac{\square}{\square}$.   Reciprocal: $\frac{\square}{\square}$.

3. $4\frac{1}{3} = \frac{\square}{\square}$.   Reciprocal: $\frac{\square}{\square}$.

4. $1\frac{5}{8} = \frac{\square}{\square}$.   Reciprocal: $\frac{\square}{\square}$.

Divide. Write each quotient in simplest form.

5. $\frac{4}{5} \div 1\frac{2}{5} = \frac{4}{5} \div \frac{\square}{5} = \frac{4}{5} \times \frac{\square}{\square} = $ _____

6. $2\frac{1}{2} \div 1\frac{3}{8} = \frac{\square}{2} \div \frac{\square}{8} = \frac{\square}{\square} \times \frac{\square}{\square} = $ _____

SKILL 18: Practice

Divide. Simplify each quotient.

1. $1\frac{4}{5} \div \frac{1}{3} =$ _____

2. $1\frac{2}{3} \div \frac{1}{8} =$ _____

3. $3\frac{4}{7} \div 3\frac{1}{2} =$ _____

4. $3\frac{4}{5} \div 1\frac{5}{7} =$ _____

5. $\frac{2}{5} \div 4\frac{3}{5} =$ _____

6. $4\frac{1}{8} \div \frac{3}{7} =$ _____

7. $2\frac{1}{2} \div 4\frac{2}{5} =$ _____

8. $2\frac{4}{5} \div 7 =$ _____

9. $\frac{5}{6} \div 1\frac{3}{4} =$ _____

10. $\frac{1}{3} \div 2\frac{1}{6} =$ _____

11. $1\frac{4}{9} \div \frac{6}{7} =$ _____

12. $1\frac{3}{4} \div \frac{4}{5} =$ _____

13. $5 \div 3\frac{1}{4} =$ _____

14. $2\frac{1}{4} \div 3\frac{4}{9} =$ _____

15. $4\frac{2}{7} \div 1\frac{1}{6} =$ _____

16. $\frac{8}{9} \div 2\frac{5}{7} =$ _____

17. $1\frac{1}{4} \div 2\frac{2}{3} =$ _____

18. $\frac{1}{4} \div 1\frac{5}{9} =$ _____

19. $2\frac{1}{4} \div 2\frac{1}{4} =$ _____

20. $1\frac{7}{8} \div 1\frac{1}{4} =$ _____

21. $1\frac{3}{4} \div \frac{1}{5} =$ _____

22. $4\frac{2}{7} \div 1\frac{1}{2} =$ _____

23. $5\frac{1}{7} \div 2\frac{1}{2} =$ _____

24. $1\frac{1}{9} \div 3 =$ _____

25. $1 \div 3\frac{5}{7} =$ _____

26. $1\frac{1}{3} \div 1\frac{2}{3} =$ _____

27. $1\frac{1}{2} \div 2\frac{3}{4} =$ _____

Solve.

28. Tom made $2\frac{1}{2}$ batches of cookies. He used $6\frac{2}{3}$ cups of flour. How much flour is used to make 1 batch?

_____

29. Sonya has $3\frac{1}{3}$ yards of fabric that she wants to cut into 6 pieces of the same length. How long should she cut each piece?

_____

30. Find $1\frac{1}{6} \div 2\frac{3}{4}$ in simplest form.

Skill 18

   A $\frac{7}{11}$ C $2\frac{5}{14}$

   B $\frac{14}{33}$ D $3\frac{5}{24}$

31. Find $8\frac{1}{5} - 6\frac{3}{5}$ in simplest form.

Skill 6

   F $1\frac{2}{5}$ H $2\frac{2}{5}$

   G $1\frac{3}{5}$ J $2\frac{3}{5}$

Section C: Dividing Fractions

SKILL 19: PROBLEM SOLVING: Operations with Fractions and Mixed Numbers

When you solve problems with fractions and mixed numbers,
you will have to choose the operations needed to solve the problem.

Example

**Renee uses $2\frac{2}{3}$ packets of seeds to plant 4 rows of corn.
What fraction of a single packet did she use to plant one row?**

Read Renee uses $2\frac{2}{3}$ packets of seeds to plant 4 rows of corn.

Plan Divide the number of packets of seeds used by the number
of rows of corn Renee planted.

Solve $2\frac{2}{3} \div 4 = \frac{8}{3} \div \frac{4}{1}$

$= \frac{8}{3} \times \frac{1}{4}$

$= \frac{8}{12}$

$= \frac{2}{3}$

Renee used $\frac{2}{3}$ packet of seeds to plant one row.

Look Back Estimate the quotient to decide whether the answer
is reasonable. Round $\frac{2}{3}$ to 1, so $2\frac{2}{3}$ rounds to 3.
Estimate $2\frac{2}{3} \div 4$ as $3 \div 4 = \frac{3}{4}$.
Since $\frac{2}{3}$ is close to $\frac{3}{4}$, the answer is reasonable.

Guided Practice

1. Cassie planted 9 rows of lettuce with $4\frac{1}{2}$ packets of seeds.
   How many rows did she plant with each packet of seeds?

   a. How can you find the number of rows she plants with
   each packet of seeds?

   _____

   b. Solve the problem. _____

2. Dave used one packet of cucumber seeds to sow $\frac{5}{8}$ row of
   cucumbers. How many rows of cucumbers can he plant
   with 4 packets of seeds?

   a. How can you find the total number of rows? _____

   _____

   b. Solve the problem. _____

SKILL 19: Practice

Solve each problem.

1. A recipe for papaya ice cream calls for $\frac{1}{4}$ cup of lemon juice and $1\frac{1}{2}$ cups of ripe papaya. How much of each ingredient is needed to make $\frac{1}{2}$ of the recipe? _____

2. There are 48 people who have signed up to attend the midnight barbecue at the Rainbow Canyon Recreation Center. The chef wants to make enough burgers so that each person can have $1\frac{1}{2}$ burgers.
   a. How many burgers should he make? _____
   b. He uses $\frac{1}{4}$ pound of beef in each burger. How much ground beef should he order? _____

3. Marvin can do one load of laundry with $\frac{1}{16}$ box of laundry detergent. How many loads of laundry can he wash with 4 boxes of the detergent? _____

4. Adriana cuts 4 apples into eighths and 3 pears into sixths to make a fruit salad. How many pieces of apple and pear does she have in the salad? _____

5. There are 12 swings at the park. Of the swings, $\frac{3}{4}$ have plastic seats. One third of the plastic seats are green. How many of the swings have green seats? _____

6. Pietro used an eight-foot board to cut 3 shelves. Each shelf was $2\frac{1}{2}$ feet long.
   a. How much board did the 3 shelves use? _____

   b. How much, if any, wood did Pietro have left? _____

TEST PREP

7. Melissa has a piece of ribbon that is $1\frac{2}{3}$ feet long. She wants to cut it into 10 pieces, each the same length. How long should she cut each piece of the ribbon?

   Skill 19

   A $\frac{1}{6}$ ft   **C** $\frac{1}{3}$ ft

   B $\frac{1}{5}$ ft   **D** 6 ft

8. Austin takes 1 quart of water on his hike. He drinks $\frac{1}{3}$ of the water going up the trail. He drinks $\frac{1}{4}$ of the water when he stops for lunch. How much water does he have left?

   Skill 8

   F $\frac{2}{7}$ qt   **H** $\frac{5}{12}$ qt

   G $\frac{5}{7}$ qt   **J** $\frac{7}{12}$ qt

Circle each correct answer.

1. Find $9 \div \frac{3}{8}$ in simplest form.

Skill 15

A $\frac{1}{24}$ **C** 12

B $3\frac{3}{8}$ **D** 24

2. Find $3\frac{1}{2} \div 1\frac{3}{4}$ in simplest form.

Skill 18

F $\frac{1}{2}$ **H** 2

G $1\frac{1}{7}$ **J** $6\frac{1}{8}$

3. Estimate: $8\frac{7}{10} \div 3\frac{1}{3}$.

Skill 14

A 2   **C** 4

B 3   **D** 5

4. Find $\frac{2}{3} \div \frac{4}{7}$ in simplest form.

Skill 16

F $\frac{8}{21}$ **H** $1\frac{1}{6}$

G $\frac{6}{7}$ **J** $1\frac{1}{2}$

5. A chef cuts 3 pans of lasagna into eighths. How many servings does he have?

Skill 19

A $\frac{3}{8}$ **C** 8

B $3\frac{3}{8}$ **D** 24

6. Find $\frac{4}{9} \div 8$ in simplest form.

Skill 17

F $\frac{1}{36}$ **H** $3\frac{5}{9}$

G $\frac{1}{18}$ **J** 18

7. Find $\frac{3}{4} \div \frac{7}{8}$ in simplest form.

Skill 16

A $\frac{4}{7}$ **C** $\frac{21}{32}$

B $\frac{6}{7}$ **D** $\frac{5}{6}$

8. Find $2\frac{1}{3} \div 1\frac{5}{6}$ in simplest form.

Skill 18

F $\frac{11}{14}$ **H** $1\frac{7}{11}$

G $1\frac{3}{11}$ **J** $4\frac{5}{18}$

9. Estimate: $4\frac{7}{8} \div \frac{9}{10}$.

Skill 14

A 2   **C** 4

B 3   **D** 5

10. Find $\frac{3}{8} \div 12$ in simplest form.

Skill 17

F $\frac{1}{32}$ **H** $4\frac{1}{2}$

G $\frac{1}{4}$ **J** 32

11. What is the reciprocal of $3\frac{1}{2}$?

Skill 18

A $\frac{6}{2}$ **C** $\frac{2}{7}$

B $\frac{7}{2}$ **D** $\frac{2}{6}$

12. Find $6 \div \frac{1}{5}$ in simplest form.

Skill 15

F $\frac{5}{6}$ **H** $\frac{1}{30}$

G $1\frac{1}{5}$ **J** 30

Mixed Review for Section C

What kind of cartoons do they watch at the beach?

To find the answer to the riddle, first find the answer to each exercise. Write each answer in simplest form. At the bottom of the page, write the letter on the blank above the answer. Some answers are not used.

E   **1.** $1\frac{1}{2} \div 1\frac{2}{3} =$ _____

L   **2.** $2\frac{1}{4} \div \frac{5}{6} =$ _____

T   **3.** $\frac{2}{3} \div \frac{4}{7} =$ _____

E   **4.** $\frac{4}{7} \div 6 =$ _____

M   **5.** $3 \div \frac{1}{8} =$ _____

U   **6.** $\frac{1}{12} \div \frac{3}{8} =$ _____

U   **7.** $3\frac{1}{5} \div 1\frac{1}{3} =$ _____

P   **8.** $\frac{3}{5} \div 9 =$ _____

C   **9.** $12 \div \frac{2}{3} =$ _____

D   **10.** $\frac{4}{9} \div \frac{2}{3} =$ _____

S   **11.** $\frac{2}{3} \div \frac{8}{9} =$ _____

A   **12.** $\frac{5}{6} \div 10 =$ _____

N   **13.** $15 \div 1\frac{2}{3} =$ _____

Y   **14.** $\frac{1}{2} \div 7 =$ _____

T   **15.** $1\frac{1}{6} \div 1\frac{3}{5} =$ _____

N   **16.** $18 \div 1\frac{1}{3} =$ _____

___ ___ ___ ___ ___   ___ ___ ___ ___ ___
$\frac{2}{3}$ $\frac{2}{9}$ 9 $\frac{9}{10}$ $\frac{1}{14}$ $\frac{35}{48}$ $2\frac{2}{5}$ $13\frac{1}{2}$ $\frac{2}{21}$ $\frac{3}{4}$